RONDE AND TIKI
BARBER

FOOTBALL STARS

Bridget Heos

New York

For the football guys in my family: My dad, my brothers Luke and Josh, sons Johnny and Richie, nephew R. J., and cousins Patrick, Danny, Jack, Kevin, and Eli (Orpin, not Manning)

Published in 2010 by The Rosen Publishing Group, Inc.
29 East 21st Street, New York, NY 10010

Library of Congress Cataloging-in-Publication Data

Heos, Bridget.
Ronde and Tiki Barber: football stars / Bridget Heos.—1st ed.
    p. cm.—(Sports families)
Includes bibliographical references and index.
ISBN 978-1-4358-3553-5 (library binding)
ISBN 978-1-4358-8510-3 (pbk)
ISBN 978-1-4358-8511-0 (6 pack)
1. Barber, Ronde, 1975-—Juvenile literature. 2. Barber, Tiki, 1975-—Juvenile literature. 3. Football players—United States—Biography—Juvenile literature. 4. Brothers—United States—Biography—Juvenile literature. I. Title.
GV939.A1H37 2010
796.3320922—dc22
[B]

2009015658

Manufactured in the United States of America

CPSIA Compliance Information: Batch #LW10YA: For Further Information contact Rosen Publishing, New York, New York at 1-800-237-9932

On the cover: Ronde and Tiki Barber talk after an October 29, 2006, game in which the Giants defeated the Buccaneers 17–3. Though occasionally rivals on the field, the identical twin brothers have always been best friends.

On the back cover: NASCAR is a registered trademark of the National Association for Stock Car Auto Racing, Inc.

Contents

As identical twins, Ronde and Tiki Barber look, well, identical. But each has a unique personality and set of football skills. Here, they're pictured at the March 15, 2006, "Hollywood Meets Motown" benefit.

Tiki and Ronde Barber took the field on

November 24, 2003, looking identical except for their uniforms. Tiki wore Giants blue; Ronde wore Buccaneers red. That day, they were not only brothers but opponents, too. In fact, one was charged with guarding the other. Ronde, a cornerback, needed to stop Tiki, the Giants' running back, from gaining too many yards.

The two had met as opponents before, but it was at the beginning of their careers, when they were barely playing. Now, both were powerhouses—Ronde as one of the best defensive players in the NFL, and Tiki as a top offensive player.

Their mother, Geraldine, watched worriedly from the stands, sitting on the Tampa Bay Buccaneers side because they were the home team. While she never missed a game, she didn't like to see her boys roughed up by opponents—especially when the opponents were each other! Their wives and children also cheered on their father and uncle in the battle of the Barbers.

Ronde showed no mercy for his brother. At one point, he tackled Tiki so hard that Tiki jumped up and asked, "What's up bro?"

Ronde said he was just doing his job. He added that if Tiki were the defensive player, he'd do the exact same thing.

In the end, Ronde won the contest, achieving 5 tackles and holding Tiki to just 55 yards on 13 carries, well below his game average. Tampa Bay won 19–13.

It would be three years before the brothers met again on the field, but Tiki hadn't forgotten his brother's hits. In the next meeting, he got back at his brother by deflecting his tackles and helping the New York Giants beat the Bucs 17–3.

Chapter One

BROTHERLY LOVE

Clashes on the football field were part of Ronde and Tiki Barber's jobs. Growing up, however, the twins were drawn together by a different force—brotherly love.

Born on April 7, 1975, in Blacksburg, Virginia, Ronde came first, followed by Tiki. From the beginning, they were drawn together like puppies. As toddlers, their mother would place them on opposite sides of the bed at night. Within minutes, one would be asleep on top of the other.

They were close in every way. They shared a bedroom. They shared clothes. They shared appearances. (As identical twins, only their mother could tell them apart.) Rather than tattling on each other, they even shared the blame when one of them did something wrong.

Although they were friends, they also competed fiercely. Since neither would surrender while behind, their games would go on forever—or at least until they were too worn out to make another move.

The fact that they could play sports at all came as a surprise to their mother. She'd been told that Ronde and Tiki would never play contact sports. Since they were born prematurely, they suffered from seizures and lung ailments as babies.

Defying doctors' predictions, the two grew to be not only healthy but also extremely athletic. Before focusing exclusively on football, they wrestled, played baseball, and ran track. No matter what they did, they'd try to outdo each other.

Ronde Barber plays cornerback. When his team, the Tampa Bay Buccaneers, played the New York Giants, as they did in this October 29, 2006, game, one of Ronde's jobs was to tackle Tiki Barber, who played running back.

One time while bike riding, Tiki wanted to prove himself braver than Ronde. He rode down a steep hill, crashed, and injured his knee.

It was baseball season, and he had to sit out because he couldn't even bend the joint. Ronde said he would play for both of them, and after each game, he came home and told Tiki what happened. That way, Tiki still felt like part of their team.

Tiki has said that when growing up in a predominately white neighborhood in Roanoke, Virginia, he and Ronde took comfort in being together. They were shy, but they understood each other. In fact, they had a secret language that, to the outside world, sounded like mumbling. To this day,

Until they were drafted into the NFL, Ronde, left, and Tiki, right, had always played on the same team. Before a November 9, 1996, game, the two Virginia Cavaliers players walked onto the field with their mother, Geraldine.

they sometimes communicate this way, and nobody else knows what they're saying.

While they both wanted to be the best in school and in sports, they wanted their brother to be the best, too. In a *Reader's Digest* interview, Tiki said, "Ronde was my teammate—he was always my teammate because Mom wouldn't have it any other way. She knew Ronde and I had this amazing bond."

Their mother, Geraldine Barber, played an important role in their lives. She and their father (who had been a football player at Virginia Tech) divorced when Ronde and Tiki were four years old. After that, he was no longer around. To support the family, Geraldine worked several jobs, still making it to all of her sons' games.

In addition to stressing the importance of family, she emphasized the need to get a good education. It wasn't tough to impress that value upon her sons, who enjoyed reading and were as competitive in school as they were in sports. Tiki graduated as valedictorian of his high school class. While Ronde was the more laid-back student, he earned good grades, too.

Besides being good athletes and students, Ronde and Tiki were good kids. They acted as each other's conscience. If one had a plan to skip school, the other would call it a terrible idea. Their mother worked a lot, so they had plenty of free time, but they spent it playing sports, doing homework, or watching movies with their girlfriends and friends.

FOOTBALL: TWIN TALENTS, DIFFERENT PERSONALITIES

Because Ronde and Tiki are identical twins, their DNA is almost identical. That means, physically, they are practically the same person. However, both agree that Ronde is the more outgoing, fun-loving twin. Because he was born first, his mother named him Jamael Orondé, which means "firstborn son" in Swahili. Tiki, who came out kicking and screaming, was named Atiim Kiambu, or "fiery-tempered king." He had more of an assertive personality.

Ronde was the better athlete, while Tiki was better at school. Today, because Ronde is less worried about what people think of him and more likely to joke around, some of his friends jokingly refer to him as "the evil twin."

Growing up, Ronde and Tiki's differences were apparent on the football field. The Barbers played little league football and have written children's books based on their experiences. In *Game Day*, Tiki is the faster twin. He becomes a ball carrier. Ronde, meanwhile, blocks the defense so that Tiki can score. As any football player knows, blocking is crucial to winning a game. But blockers don't always get as much recognition as ball runners. In the book, Tiki becomes the star of the team and Ronde feels unnoticed. At the end of the book, Tiki helps Ronde understand that he's important to the team, too.

Tiki has said that in real life, Ronde eventually became a top scorer, too. In fact, Tiki said that in many things, he started out being the more talented twin, only to be surpassed by Ronde down the road.

Though different in some ways, the twins shared one characteristic. By age ten, both were powerhouses on the field. Tiki gracefully ran past his opponents to score, and Ronde easily tackled kids two years older than him.

By the time they got to high school, the brothers excelled at being running backs, and they vied for the position. Tiki was a little better at it, so the coach switched Ronde to safety, where he shined as a defensive player.

IDENTICAL TWINS: DID YOU KNOW?

- Identical twins come from the same fertilized egg, as opposed to two eggs, which would make them fraternal.

- While having fraternal twins can run in a family, having identical twins does not. It is pure luck.

- Some identical twins are "mirror image" twins. This happens when the egg splits late in the embryonic stage. It means some of the twins' features occur on opposite sides of their bodies. One might be left-handed, for instance, and the other right-handed.

- For a long time, scientists thought identical twins had the exact same DNA. However, recent evidence shows that while similar, their DNA differs in something called copy number variations. This explains why one twin can contract an illness such as Parkinson's disease while the other doesn't.

- Some twins have reported literally feeling each other's pain. For instance, the twin of a person who is having heart surgery might feel heart pain during the surgery.

- Ronde and Tiki, like some other twins, talk to each other in what sounds like their own language. They are speaking English, but it is in such a quiet mumble that only they can understand each other.

To this day, Tiki, like in *Game Day*, is the more well-known brother. For one thing, he played in a larger market—New York—than Ronde, who played in Tampa. Also, Tiki became more involved in the media side of things. Ronde says that people frequently mistake him for Tiki, but nobody mistakes Tiki for Ronde.

Although they are identical, Ronde Barber, left, is said to be the more easygoing twin, whereas Tiki has more of an assertive personality.

While the general public may know Tiki better, Ronde's defensive prowess hasn't gone unnoticed. ESPN called him the most complete corner-back in the league, and his teammates talk about his hard work and excellent instincts.

As for Tiki, he has often given credit to his blockers for his success, perhaps because, during their school days, his brother taught him how important that position was.

Ronde and Tiki excelled in many sports, and for awhile, football was just another game. Then, in high school, Tiki fell in love with football. He loved the feeling of outrunning everyone on the field for a touchdown. Ronde excelled in the sport, too, and by their senior year, college recruiters were calling.

They didn't ask for one twin in particular but were happy to talk to either. The twins planned on going to college together, so the recruiters were guaranteed two good players if they signed just one.

At first, the brothers enjoyed the phone calls, which came from as far away as the University of California–Los Angeles (UCLA). But when they started coming one after the other, it became too much. They'd ask their mom to tell the recruiters they weren't home.

They couldn't put off the recruiters forever, though. Soon, they had a decision to make. Which school should they attend?

Chapter Two

COLLEGE FOOTBALL: THE SCHOOL OF HARD KNOCKS

Ronde and Tiki narrowed their prospects to Michigan, UCLA, Clemson, and their home state school, the University of Virginia. Never imagining they'd play in the NFL after college, they wanted a school with great academics. That way, they'd be ready for careers in a field such as business or engineering.

They thought Clemson was too focused on athletics. Michigan, they decided, had too big of a football program and was too cold. UCLA was too far from home. Virginia, on the other hand, was just right.

There, they were impressed when they spoke to a football player who was also a top nuclear engineering student. They felt that football wasn't a huge deal at the school, and football players were treated like everybody else. Ronde and Tiki would be able to play the game while being regular college students.

They moved from their mother's home to the school, where they lived as roommates. Their first season of college football wasn't great. Ronde was redshirted, meaning he practiced but didn't play games. That way, he would be able to play football for five years of college. Tiki played in games, but not much.

During this time, they listened to their coaches and worked hard. The next year, things were looking up—for Ronde at least. No longer redshirted,

Tiki's breakout season for the Virginia Cavaliers was 1995. Here, he carries the ball in a winning game against the Maryland Terrapins on November 11, 1995.

he became a breakout star his sophomore year. He had the second most interceptions among college players in America—10 for the year—and was named Atlantic Coast Rookie of the Year.

Tiki still wasn't a star running back. In fact, he was having better luck in track and field. He competed in the long jump and dreamed of being in the Olympics. But his coach told him that in order to step up his football game junior year, he'd need to gain 15 pounds (7 kilograms)—not good for long jumping. Tiki had a choice: the long jump or football.

After his team's Super Bowl XXXVII victory on January 26, 2003, Ronde Barber celebrated with his mother and Tiki. The Buccaneers defeated the Raiders 48–21.

He chose football. Those 15 pounds of muscle paid off for Tiki during his junior year, and Ronde continued to be a defensive powerhouse. The Virginia Cavaliers had a great season and played their final game against the Florida State Seminoles, the number-one team in the nation.

Since it was a home game, the stands were packed with students cheering in the pouring rain. The Cavaliers were winning 33–28 during the final play. The Seminoles tricked the Cavaliers by snapping the ball to a player other than the quarterback. He ran for the end zone. Seemingly destined to clinch the game for Florida State, he was stopped just 1 foot (0.3 meters) away from a touchdown when a Cavalier pounded the ball out of his hands. The referee called it a fumble, and Ronde and Tiki's team won. The crowd rushed the field. It was a high point in their college careers.

Later that year, Ronde and Tiki suffered a blow. They found out that their mother had breast cancer. During their senior season, she underwent both surgery and chemotherapy. It was a scary time for the family. But through it all, she never missed a game. Her sons called her every day, sometimes telling her to rest, other times encouraging her to keep busy so that she wouldn't feel depressed.

Their mother made it through the treatments and, today, is cancer free and a volunteer for the American Cancer Society.

Ronde and Tiki remained roommates for two years of college and then shared an apartment.

During that time, Tiki met a woman named Ginny. For a long time, she couldn't tell the two apart. They wore different earrings, and that was the only way she knew. Ronde's earring was round; Tiki's was a hoop. She remembered because Ronde sounded like round. Then one day, the twins stopped wearing the earrings. Eventually, Ginny could tell them apart, which was a good thing because she and Tiki went on to get married.

When Ginny and Tiki met, he wasn't the famous football star that he is today. An unknown college player, he didn't even think he'd play in the pros. But he and Ginny were both ambitious. She planned to move to New York to do public relations in the fashion design industry. By Tiki's senior year of college, he'd surpassed his own expectations. Ronde had, too. Both were going pro.

High school football players being recruited by colleges get to choose what school they attend. The National Football League (NFL) is different. Teams choose the players. Ronde and Tiki didn't know where they would end up, but they were pretty sure they wouldn't be on the same team.

On the day of the 1997 draft, they didn't gather with a big group to await the results, as many players do. Instead, they went golfing together, their cell phones in their pockets.

Tiki got the call first. The New York Giants' coach, Jim Fassel, phoned to tell Tiki he would be the Giants' second-round draft pick. It was good news for him because Ginny planned to move to New York the following year, when she graduated from college.

Ronde was next. In the third round, the Tampa Bay Buccaneers selected him as a cornerback. For the first time, Ronde and Tiki would be living not only in different cities but also on opposite ends of the East Coast. They were both drafted to the National Football Conference (NFC) conference, meaning they would play games together in the regular season, but they'd be on opposite sides of the field.

It was a tough time to be apart. After all, the NFL isn't Disneyland. Injury and competition weed out most players after just a few years. The Barbers knew a short-lived football career was a possibility. Would they

Former Giants coach Jim Fassel called Tiki the day of the 1997 draft to tell him he'd be the team's second-round draft pick. It was good news for Tiki because his future wife, Ginny, had career plans in New York.

successfully navigate their first years in the league, especially without being teammates?

GOING THE DISTANCE

Ronde and Tiki's pro careers were shaky in the beginning. During Ronde's rookie year, he played just one game.

Tiki started in five games, but then he tore the posterior cruciate ligament in his right knee. After being out for four weeks, he played again, but not as a starter. Instead, he became a punt returner and third-down specialist, meaning he didn't play first, second, or fourth downs. Tiki wished he could start, but he knew it wasn't in the cards right then. Instead, he vowed to be the best punt returner and third-down player in the league.

The Barbers wanted to prove themselves. They both wanted to start. Unfortunately, with the following year's draft, their prospects became more doubtful.

In 1998, the Buccaneers selected a new cornerback, probably to fill the starting position. If Ronde wanted to start, he needed to prove himself the best man for the job. In the nine games Ronde started that year, he did just that. He became a powerful blitzer, sacking quarterbacks when they least expected it.

Tiki faced tough competition after the 2000 draft. When the Giants drafted Heisman Trophy–winner Ron Dayne in the first round, fans assumed he'd become the starting running back. But Tiki was determined to break out of his third-down role that year. In fact, he told teammates he would start that year. In the off-season, he woke up early to run hill repeats. At practice, he always did his best.

His hard work and competitive spirit paid off. Including the postseason, he started in 14 games, rushed for 1,159 yards, and caught 83 passes. Dayne ended up starting, too; he and Tiki took turns. Because Dayne was bigger, he was nicknamed "Thunder." Tiki, who was faster, was called "Lightning."

Tiki and the Giants played so well that, by the end of the 2000 season, they were bound for the playoffs. However, sports reporters didn't have

SIMILARITIES AND DIFFERENCES

SAME:

- Both are married with two children the same age (Tiki has boys; Ronde has girls).
- Both have radio and TV experience. Tiki is a full-time journalist. Ronde has hosted radio and TV football shows, and appeared in ads.
- Both have been named one of *People* magazine's "50 most beautiful people."
- Both Ronde's wife, Claudia, and Tiki's wife, Ginny, work in the field of marketing.

DIFFERENT:

- Ronde was born a few minutes earlier than Tiki.
- Ronde weighs less than Tiki.
- Tiki lives in New York. Ronde lives in Tampa Bay, Florida.
- Tiki hobnobs with politicians and power brokers in New York. Ronde enjoys a laid-back lifestyle involving golfing in Florida.
- Tiki wears Italian suits. Ronde wears casual clothing.
- Tiki is now retired from football. Ronde still plays.
- As a cornerback, Ronde plays defense. Tiki, a running back, played offense.
- Ronde is number 20. Tiki was number 21.

high hopes for the team. Some even referred to them as the worst team ever to make it to a conference championship. Undaunted, Tiki played his heart out in the playoff games, even though he had a broken arm. (He wore a soft cast so that he could participate.) Defying predictions, his team defeated the Vikings 41–0 in a game known as "forty-one-doughnut."

In 2000, Tiki faced tough competition from his teammate, Heisman Trophy winner Ron Dayne, pictured on December 23, 2000, in a winning game against the Jaguars. He and Tiki both started in different games that season.

After the game, the Giants president and co-CEO, Wellington Mara, jokingly told the press, "In two weeks, we're going to try to become the worst team ever to win the Super Bowl."

Tiki's team didn't win Super Bowl XXXV, though. They didn't even play well.

And by the end of the season, Tiki faced a new challenge. Even though he was a tremendous rusher, he also led the league in fumbling. Would that overshadow the records he was setting for yards gained?

Chapter Three

OVERCOMING CHALLENGES

In 2000, Tiki fumbled nine times. In 2001, he fumbled eight times. And in both 2002 and 2003, he fumbled nine times. During the same seasons, Tiki excelled at other things. He carried the ball more than two hundred times and averaged more than 1,500 yards per season. That made him one of the league's premier running backs. But Tiki knew that fumbling the ball could cost his team a game.

Tiki's best and worst game was on December 28, 2002, when he gained a phenomenal 203 rushing yards but fumbled three times. With the game tied and the playoffs on the line, he fumbled in the fourth quarter, giving the Philadelphia Eagles the chance to win the game with a field goal. Amazingly, their ace kicker missed. The game went into overtime, and the Giants won with a field goal. Relieved that he hadn't cost his team a trip to the playoffs, Tiki broke down and cried.

After the game, he and Ronde talked. Ronde told Tiki, "You almost had millions of New Yorkers ready to kill you."

Although Ronde was just giving Tiki a hard time, the statement was pretty accurate. Tiki's home team was unforgiving. The crowd booed him on his home field and sang, "Fumbleaya."

Tiki felt horrible.

It wasn't just his fumbles that kept the Giants from the playoffs, however. Though they were a good team, the Giants were seemingly cursed.

Their coach at the time, Jim Fassel, remarked in the *New York Daily News*: "It seems like we find a different way [to lose] every time."

Ronde tried to encourage Tiki through it all. After losing a game on January 5, 2003, that would have sent the Giants to the playoffs as a wild-card, Tiki called Ronde.

"Don't worry about all this garbage," Ronde told him. "You had a great season, and I know it."

At the same time, Ronde gave Tiki a hard time. Ronde was on his way to the Super Bowl. Appearing as a guest on Tiki's radio show, Ronde vowed to win the game, saying, "We're going to do what you guys couldn't do."

Ronde's star was rising. A stealth player who would come out of nowhere to sack quarterbacks and intercept passes, he'd been racking up impressive stats year after year.

In 2000, he scored on both a fumble return and an interception return, one of only three players in Buccaneers history to do so. In 2001, he caught 10 interceptions—his career record. During the 2002 postseason, he led the Buccaneers to an NFC championship by getting a quarterback sack, forcing a fumble, and later intercepting the ball for a 92-yard touchdown. Playing in Super Bowl XXXVII against Oakland on January 26, 2003, Ronde got 4 tackles and earned a championship ring.

Tiki, who had traveled to the game to watch his brother, was very proud.

Soon, things were looking up for Tiki, too. In 2004, his new coach, Tom Coughlin, showed him a new way to hold the ball, by holding his wrist with his left hand so that the other team, aware of Tiki's weakness, couldn't jab it out of his hands.

The coach also sent him to strength training. Soon, Tiki was leg pressing 1,100 pounds (499 kg). His weight trainer had also helped him to believe in himself again. Tiki never thought he'd be able to lift that much weight. Joe Carini, the weight trainer, thought differently. He'd say, "Come on, Tiki! You've got to get your mind right. We're gonna do this."

Tiki, already an offensive force, came into the 2004 season physically and mentally ready to confront the defense. Ronde was coming off a

Ronde and teammate Shelton Quarles tackle Jerry Porter of the Oakland Raiders during Super Bowl XXXVII. Ronde is known for his ability to read offensive players.

Super Bowl win. At the height of their careers, the brothers took the league by storm.

RONDE: A QUARTERBACK'S WORST NIGHTMARE

Ronde became known for seemingly reading players' minds. He could predict where a quarterback's pass would go and beat the offensive player there. In the NFL, this has resulted in 23 career sacks and 37 interceptions, well exceeding the 20 sacks/20 interceptions mark that no other cornerback in NFL history has surpassed. Now, he's well on his way to the 30/40 mark.

In a July 23, 2001, *Sports Illustrated* article, Ronde's teammate and fellow cornerback Donnie Abraham described Ronde's blitzing prowess: "He always seems to find the seam. Somehow he squeezes through 300-pound [136 kg] offensive linemen and makes plays. Every blitz he goes on, he thinks he's going to get to the quarterback. It's always full speed with him."

Getting sacks has become increasingly difficult since offenses now know to stop Ronde's blitzes. Ronde continues to make his mark in other ways, though. In terms of playmaking, he is one of three players in NFL history to score 11 touchdowns on interceptions or fumble returns. He is the second player in Buccaneers history to score three different ways: through a punt return, fumble return, and interception. He also holds the team record for career interceptions. In 2001 and 2005, he broke the team record for the most interceptions in a single game. In both cases, he intercepted three times against the New Orleans Saints. Then, during an October 22, 2006, game against the Philadelphia Eagles, he scored 2 touchdowns on interceptions, the first player in team history to do so.

Ronde is good at intercepting because he beats players to wherever they plan to go. Once there, he either blocks the pass or intercepts it. It's not that Ronde has ESP. Rather, he spends hours watching footage of games, gets a sense of where players move, and then takes educated guesses as to where the ball is going.

Ronde has 12 career defensive touchdowns. Here, he scores a touchdown on an interception during a winning game against the Philadelphia Eagles on October 22, 2006.

In addition to scoring touchdowns, Ronde is a tough tackler. During each of the five seasons, he's completed an impressive 100 tackles. In 2005, he broke his own team record by completing 120 tackles.

Some of his career stats include 1,065 tackles, 37 interceptions, 23 sacks, 10 forced fumbles, and 198 defended passes, and in the postseason, 50 tackles, 2 interceptions, 1 sack, 1 forced fumble, and 11 passes defended.

Tiki retired from playing football to become a correspondent for the NBC television show *Today*. Cohosts Meredith Viera and Matt Lauer, and anchor Ann Curry, greeted him on his first day, April 16, 2007.

It's no wonder Ronde's been named to the NFL Pro Bowl five times, has started in 168 regular-season games, and holds a Super Bowl XXXVII ring.

While wearing a Super Bowl ring is a huge accomplishment, Ronde has said that his best on-field moment occurred in the playoff game before the Super Bowl, during which his 92-yard interception return clinched the playoff game.

TIKI: LEGENDARY RUSHER

In 2004, Tiki scored a career-high 13 touchdowns and gained 1,518 rushing yards. The next year, he beat his own record, rushing for 1,860 yards and becoming the first player in NFL history to gain 1,800 rushing yards and 500 receiving yards in one season. He finished his career with 55 touchdowns, 10,449 rushing yards (a Giants team record), and 2,217 carries, averaging 4.7 yards per carry. In his final regular-season game, Tiki rushed for 234 yards, another team record. In fact, he smashed most New York Giants' offensive records during his tenure with the team.

The formula for Tiki's success was simple: he was smart, fast, and tough. At times, cornerbacks would bounce off him. When he did go down, he'd jump back up, smiling. He didn't want his opponents to know they'd hurt him. That way, on their next tackle, they'd try to tackle him harder and would likely overdo it and mess up.

When Tiki retired after the 2006 season, he was on top of his game, with more yards gained

SIDE-BY-SIDE STATS

RONDE	TIKI
HEIGHT/WEIGHT	**HEIGHT/WEIGHT**
5'10", 184 pounds	5'10", 205 pounds
SEASONS	**SEASONS**
13	10
CAREER STARTS IN REGULAR-SEASON GAMES	**CAREER STARTS IN REGULAR-SEASON GAMES**
168	109
TOUCHDOWNS	**TOUCHDOWNS**
12 (defensive)	55
TEAM RECORDS (OF SEVERAL)	**TEAM RECORDS (OF SEVERAL)**
Most tackles for a cornerback, 1,065	All-time career rushing yards, 10,449
NFC CHAMPIONSHIPS	**NFC CHAMPIONSHIPS**
2002 season	2000 season
SUPER BOWLS	**SUPER BOWLS**
Ronde's Buccaneers won Super Bowl XXXVII	Tiki's Giants lost Super Bowl XXXV

in the past three years than anyone else in the NFL. He'd been named to three Pro Bowls. He didn't have a Super Bowl ring, but he had played in the championship. Feeling like he'd reached the pinnacle of his football potential, he decided to try a new career: TV journalism.

Ronde, on the other hand, had no intention of retiring. He still loved the game. What would it be like for him now that Tiki, his longtime supporter and competitor, was no longer in the league?

Chapter Four

Traveling Separate Paths Again

Tiki retired for several reasons. For one thing, he could feel the fire in him cooling. He knew that with age, he'd lost a step, resulting in shorter yard gains during carries. Fans didn't notice, but he knew. Tiki had watched other football stars stay in the game too long. He didn't want to become a has-been. He thought it was better to be remembered for being on top of his game.

Also, running backs get pummeled game after game. They last in the league an average of two-and-a-half years compared to less than four years for all players in the league. As a rookie, Tiki would recover from a Sunday game by Wednesday; it now took him until Friday night.

Finally, Tiki has said that Tom Coughlin, the new coach, had a different style than his former coach, Jim Fassel, who Tiki had worked well with. Fassel was a motivator, a guy who got excited about the game, shared his enthusiasm with his players, and treated them like colleagues.

Coughlin, on the other hand, was a disciplinarian. He had more of an "I'm your coach, do what I say," attitude. That worked for some players. But for a veteran like Tiki, who was feeling the hits of ten years in the game, it didn't.

In his book *Tiki: My Life in the Game and Beyond*, Tiki acknowledged that Coughlin helped him solve his fumbling problem and that during the coach's tenure, his stats were better than ever. However, he said, "He robbed me of the joy I felt playing football. I had lost that. He had taken it away."

For those reasons, Tiki decided to retire. When he announced it during the 2006 season, fans turned on him, just as they had during his fumbling years. They said he was a distraction to the team for speaking his mind, criticizing his coach at times, and announcing his retirement before the season's end. Tiki said that he had never signed on to the NFL to keep his mouth shut and play. Rather, he reserved the right to speak his mind.

Ronde and Tiki played their last football game together on October 29, 2006, after which the brothers shared a friendly moment. The Giants defeated the Buccaneers 17–3.

Still, fans considered him a deserter.

Tiki and Ronde played football against each other just one more time on October 29, 2006. The last time they'd played, Ronde had outplayed Tiki. This time, Tiki dodged or deflected most of Ronde's tackles. In the end, the Giants won.

With a solid regular-season record, Tiki hoped to end his career with another run for the Super Bowl. Unfortunately, the team lost in its first playoff game. Tiki retired and embarked on a new career as a journalist.

WHERE THEY ARE NOW

Tiki already had radio and television experience. In fact, he and Ronde had shared a satellite radio show called *The Barber Shop*. Just as Ronde is

Tiki paused for a photo during his first day on the set of *Today*. In addition to covering news stories, he is a sports analyst on NBC's *Football Night in America*.

known for watching game films to become a better football player, he carefully researched the material for the show and knew his stuff. Tiki was the color commentator.

Tiki always said he wanted to further his broadcasting career, and after retiring from football, he went to work for NBC. Lots of NFL players become football commentators, but Tiki also became a news correspondent on *The Today Show*. He's covered topics ranging from the tragic Virginia Tech shootings to the Beijing Olympics.

He is also a commentator on *Football Night*, which airs after NFL games. Since his retirement, Tiki has been called out by other former

FROM FOOTBALL PLAYERS TO AUTHORS

Tiki and Ronde have written several children's books based on their experiences of playing football as kids.

Teammates tells the story of Tiki fumbling the ball and his brother setting up secret early-morning practices to help him overcome this.

By My Brother's Side talks about a bike accident and the brothers' joy when Tiki could finally play sports with Ronde again.

Go Long! is about a grade school team's reaction to their coach leaving and the science teacher filling his shoes.

Kickoff! describes the boys' transition from elementary school to junior high ball.

Their sixth book, *Wild Card,* is a middle grade novel.

players-turned-sports analysts for criticizing his old team. Tiki said Tom Coughlin was difficult to work for and quarterback Eli Manning lacked leadership. While other commentators had said similar things, they said that Tiki, as a former Giants player, should show some loyalty.

Tiki defended himself, saying it would be cowardly to shy away from the issue of Coughlin and how he contributed to his early retirement. As for Manning, Tiki said it was his job to tell things as he saw them. Ultimately, the Giants won the Super Bowl that season, and some credit Tiki's statements, in part, for getting Manning fired up to lead his team to victory.

Today, Tiki lives in a large Manhattan apartment with his wife, Ginny, and their two sons, A. J. and Chason. Though New York fans have sometimes given Tiki a hard time, they also see him as one of the greatest Giants players of all time. A Manhattan ice cream parlor even named a flavor after him. Called Tiki-tacchio, it is vanilla ice cream with M&Ms, chocolate chunks, and pistachios.

Ronde still plays football. He has said that it was hard, at first, to play in the NFL without Tiki because watching his brother play on Sundays was a big motivator for him. Ronde and Tiki had played football most of their lives. Whether side-by-side or on opposite sides of the field, they encouraged each other, cheered for each other, and sometimes got on each other's case.

When Tiki was fumbling, Ronde told him he needed to take care of the problem. Once, when Ronde tried to pick up a blocked punt on the run rather than falling on it, Tiki told him over the phone, "That'll learn 'ya. Next time, fall on the ball."

Now, Ronde has gotten used to being the only Barber twin in the NFL and says he doesn't plan to quit anytime soon. He still loves the game—even the daily grind of going to practice.

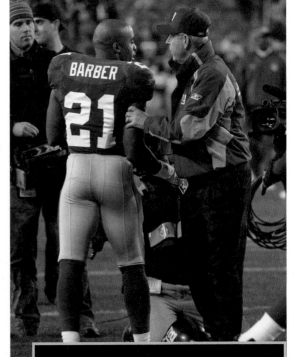

New York Giants coach Tom Coughlin talks to Tiki before a December 30, 2006, game against the Washington Redskins.

He has signed a contract to play for the Buccaneers for several more years. He will most likely retire with the team, a prospect he finds comforting. Ronde is considered one of the best cornerbacks in the league, but he still has goals he'd like to accomplish before the end of his career.

Ronde lives in a large home on a golf course with his wife, Claudia, and their two daughters, Yammile Rose and Justyce Rosina, in Tampa Bay. He lives a more laid-back life than Tiki, who often attends parties with

Tiki, left, and Ronde, right, read their book *Kickoff!* to children from the Police Athletic League in New York City on November 6, 2007. The brothers have written a series of books based on their experiences playing sports as kids.

politicians, actors, and foreign dignitaries. Ronde prefers to play golf or have a Buccaneers teammate and his wife over for a cookout.

People say that Ronde could have survived in New York and learned to be less laid-back. However, they say Tiki would have gotten restless in Tampa because he is more of a bright lights, big city guy.

Tiki continues to say that his brother is the more athletic twin. Others would argue that Tiki is the better athlete. Still others would say the two are equally good but in different ways.

While less identical in their personalities and careers than their appearances would suggest, the Barbers remain extremely close. Though living in separate parts of the country, they always find time to talk to each other.

Currently, Ronde and Tiki are writing children's books together and touring the country to promote them. One thing that critics have said about the books is that the siblings in them care about each other and like being around each other, which is refreshing.

Tiki and Ronde have always been that way. Perhaps being a great brotherly team is what made them such great contributors to their NFL teams later in life.

TIMELINE

1975

Ronde and Tiki Barber are born in Virginia. Because they suffered from seizures as infants, their doctor said they will never be able to play contact sports. However, the boys recover from their condition and later play little league football.

1993

After playing for the Cave Springs High School Knights, Ronde and Tiki graduate and begin their college football careers as University of Virginia Cavaliers.

1995

In Ronde and Tiki's final sophomore year game, the Virginia Cavaliers upset the number-one-ranked Florida Seminoles, a game still shown on classic sports channels.

1997

Both Ronde and Tiki are drafted into the NFL: Ronde by the Tampa Bay Buccaneers and Tiki by the New York Giants.

1999

Tiki marries Ginny Cha.

2001

Ronde marries Claudia Patron. Tiki makes it to Super Bowl XXXV, but the Giants lose to the Baltimore Ravens.

2003

Ronde goes to Super Bowl XXXVII, and the Buccaneers beat the Oakland Raiders.

2004

Ronde and Tiki Barber release their children's book, *By My Brother's Side.*

2005

During the last game of the 2004 season, Tiki becomes the Giants career rushing leader, with 6,927 yards. Ronde becomes the first NFL cornerback in history to accumulate 20 career interceptions and 20 sacks. Ronde and Tiki play in their first Pro Bowl together as teammates. They are the seventh set of brothers selected to the Pro Bowl, but the first twins. Tiki appears in the off-Broadway play *Women of Manhattan*.

2006

Ronde and Tiki donate $1,000,000 to the University of Virginia to support a scholarship fund for African American students and the Young Alumni Council.

2007

After a final playoff game, Tiki retires from football and becomes a correspondent for NBC's *Today Show*.

2009

Tiki Barber founds Tiki Recreation, a playground company that creates eco-friendly and safe playground equipment for kids.

GLOSSARY

American Football Conference (AFC) One of two divisions in the NFL, consisting of sixteen teams, which formed after the American Football League merged with the National Football League.

blitz An attempt by a defensive player to break through the line and tackle the quarterback.

cornerback A defensive back positioned outside the line to guard outside running plays and wide receivers.

interception A catch by a defensive player that shifts possession from the offense to the defense.

National Football Conference (NFC) One of two divisions in the NFL, consisting of sixteen teams, which formed after the American Football League merged with the National Football League. Ronde and Tiki Barber played on NFC teams.

National Football League (NFL) A league founded in 1920 to organize teams playing professional football and standardize the rules of the game. It now consists of thirty-two teams playing in the NFC and AFC conferences.

NFC championship One of two conference championships that decide which teams will compete in the Super Bowl.

NFL draft A yearly process by which professional teams draft top college players. To balance the talent, the worst team in the NFL gets the first pick, followed by the second-worst team, etc.

passing yards Distance gained from a pass, starting at the line of scrimmage and ending wherever the receiver is down.

Pro Bowl A game in which the best players of the AFC compete against the best of the NFC. Players are determined based on coaches' and players' votes.

recruiters Members of a college football staff charged with encouraging high school seniors to play on their team.

redshirted A college player's status, meaning he'll practice but not play freshman year in order to gain a fifth year of eligibility.

running back A fullback or halfback who carries the ball either after a handoff or pass. Typically, the halfback, which Tiki was, carries the ball while the fullback blocks.

rushing yards Distance gained when an offensive player runs the ball.

Super Bowl The annual NFL championship game, deciding the best team in the league.

Canadian Football League (CFL)

50 Wellington Street, East

3rd Floor

Toronto, ON M5E 1C8

Canada

(416) 322-9650

Web site: http://www.cfl.ca

The CFL is Canada's professional football league.

Canadian Interuniversity Sport

801 King Edward, Suite N205

Ottawa, ON K1N 6N5

Canada

(613) 562-5670

Web site: http://www.universitysport.ca/e/football

This is the national program through which Canadian university teams compete against one another.

National Association of Intercollegiate Athletics (NAIA)

1200 Grand Boulevard

Kansas City, MO 64106

(816) 595-8000

Web site: http://naia.cstv.com

The NAIA is a collegiate athletic league made up of three hundred colleges and universities (generally smaller than NCAA Division I schools) and offering twenty-three championships in thirteen sports.

National Collegiate Athletic Association (NCAA)

700 W. Washington Street

P.O. Box 6222

Indianapolis, IN 46206-6222

(317) 917-6222

Web site: http://www.ncaa.org

The NCAA is an association through which college athletic teams compete, following the rules of the organization.

Pop Warner Little Scholars, Inc.

586 Middletown Boulevard, Suite C-100

Langhorne, PA 19047

(215) 752-2691

Web site: http://www.popwarner.com

This nonprofit organization provides football programs for kids five to sixteen years old.

University of Virginia

Charlottesville, VA 22904

(434) 924-0311

Web site: http://www.virginia.edu

This is the university that Ronde and Tiki Barber attended and played for.

USA Football

8300 Boone Boulevard, Suite 625

Vienna, VA 22182

(877) 536-6822

Web site: http://www.usafootball.com

USA Football is the official governing board of youth and amateur football in America.

WEB SITES

Due to the changing nature of Internet links, Rosen Publishing has developed an online list of Web sites related to the subject of this book. This site is updated regularly. Please use this link to access the list:

http://www.rosenlinks.com/sfam/barb

FOR FURTHER READING

Barber, Ronde, Tiki Barber, and Robert Burleigh. *By My Brother's Side*. New York, NY: Simon & Schuster/Paula Wiseman Books, 2004.

Barber, Ronde, Tiki Barber, and Robert Burleigh. *Game Day*. New York, NY: Simon & Schuster/Paula Wiseman Books, 2005.

Barber, Ronde, Tiki Barber, and Paul Mantell. *Kickoff!* New York, NY: Aladdin, 2008.

Barber, Ronde, Tiki Barber, and Robert Burleigh. *Teammates*. New York, NY: Simon & Schuster/Paula Wiseman Books, 2006.

Barber, Tiki, and Gil Reavill. *Tiki: My Life in the Game and Beyond*. New York, NY: Simon Spotlight Entertainment, 2007.

Green, Tim. *Football Genius*. New York, NY: HarperCollins, 2008.

Lupica, Mike. *Two-Minute Drill: Mike Lupica's Comeback Kids*. New York, NY: Philomel, 2007.

Play Football! New York, NY: DK Publishing, 2002.

1,001 Facts About Running Backs. New York, NY: DK Publishing, 2003.

BIBLIOGRAPHY

Associated Press. "NY Giants vs. Tampa Bay Recap." November 24, 2003. Retrieved February 5, 2009 (http://sports.espn.go.com/nfl/recap?gameId=231124027).

Associated Press. "Tiki's Offseason Criticisms Rallied Eli, Giants." January 26, 2008. Retrieved February 5, 2009 (http://nbcsports.msnbc.com/id/228844290).

Barber, Tiki, and Gil Reavill. *Tiki: My Life in the Game and Beyond.* New York, NY: Simon Spotlight Entertainment, 2007.

Berger, Warren. "Scoring Extra Points." *Reader's Digest.* Retrieved January 6, 2009 (http://www.rd.com/tiki-and-ronde-barber---scoring-extra-points/article26502.html).

Bradley, John Ed. "Play Mates." *Sports Illustrated*, July 23, 2001. Retrieved January 6, 2009 (http://vault.sportsillustrated.cnn.com/vault/article/magazine/MAG1023025/index.htm).

Branch, John. "The Barbers, Identical Twins, Are Not as Alike as They Look." *New York Times*, October 25, 2006. Retrieved January 6, 2009 (http://www.nytimes.com/2006/10/25/sports/football/25barber.html).

Brown, Jen. "Tiki Barber Makes 'Giant' Debut on Today." TodayShow.com, April 16, 2007. Retrieved January 29, 2008 (http://today.msnbc.msn.com/id/18123547).

Cramer, Ben. "The Power of Two." *The University of Virginia Magazine*, Spring 2006. Retrieved January 6, 2009 (http://www.uvamagazine.org/site/c.esJNK1PIJrH/b.1601293/k.9A06/The_Power_of_Two).

Gola, Hank, and Ralph Vacchiano. "Crushing Blows and Devastating Fumbles Mark Giant-Eagle Rivalry." *New York Daily News*, January 10, 2009. Retrieved January 29, 2009 (http://www.nydailynews.com/sports/football/giants/2009/01/10/2009-01-10_crushing_blows_and_devastating_fumbles_m.html).

Hack, Damon. "Pro Football: Barber Is Buccaneers' All-Purpose Apparition." *New York Times*, January 21, 2003. Retrieved January 29, 2009 (http://query.nytimes.com/gst/fullpage.html?res=9900E3DE1330F932A15752C0A9659C8B63).

HamptonRoads.com. "Tampa Bay's Ronde Barber: 'I'm Gonna Keep Plugging at It.'" Retrieved January 29, 2009 (http://hamptonroads.com/2008/12/tampa-bays-ronde-barber-im-gonna-keep-plugging-it).

Hiestand, Michael. "NBC's Barber Cut Down by Analyst Peers." *USA Today*, September 7, 2007. Retrieved February 3, 2009 (http://www.usatoday.com/sports/columnist/hiestand-tv/2007-09-060hiestand-tv-col_N.htm).

International Herald Tribune Sports. "Final Meeting for Barber Twins? Ronde Understands Tiki's Decision." October 26, 2006. Retrieved January 29, 2009 (http://www.iht.com/articles/ap/2006/10/27/sports/NA_SPT_FBL_NFL_Barber_vs_Barber.php).

Keil, Jennifer Gould. "The 21 Club." *New York Post*, March 29, 2007. Retrieved January 6, 2009 (http://www.nypost.com/seven/03292007/realestate/the_21_club_realestate_jennifer_gould_keil.htm?page=0).

O'Connor, Anahad. "Really? The Claim: Identical Twins Have Identical DNA." *New York Times*, March 11, 2008. Retrieved January 6, 2009 (http://www.nytimes.com/2008/03/11/health/11real.html).

Olney, Buster. "Pro Football; Barbers Sharing the Excitement and Mistaken Identities." *New York Times*, January 26, 2003. Retrieved January 6, 2009 (http://query.nytimes.com/gst/fullpage.html?res=9B0CE1DD1539F935A15752C0A9659C8B63).

Pasquarelli, Len. "Barber Is NFL's Most Complete Corner." ESPN.com, July 29, 2005. Retrieved January 6, 2009 (http://sports.espn.go.com/nfl/trainingcamp05/columns/story?columnist=pasquarelli_len&id=2119748).

Pedulla, Tom. "For Barbers, It's Two for the Show." *USA Today*, January 23, 2003. Retrieved January 6, 2009 (http://www.usatoday.com/sports/football/super/2003-01-23-barbers_x.htm).

SimonSays.com. "Q&A: A Conversation with Twin NFL Stars, Tiki Barber & Ronde Barber, Authors of *By My Brother's Side*." Retrieved January 6, 2009 (http://www.simonsays.com/content/destination.cfm?tab=22&pid=330638&agid=8).

Solomon, Greg. "Barber Brothers Reunited." NFL.com, February 10, 2005. Retrieved February 2, 2009 (http://giants.com/news/special_features/story.asp?story_id=5556).

USA Today. "Tiki Barber Stands by His Comments." September 7, 2007. Retrieved January 6, 2009 (http://www.usatoday.com/sports/football/2007-09-06-1217492640_x.htm).

Vacchiano, Ralph. "Get a Grip: Tiki Tired of Hearing About Last Year's Fumble-itis." *New York Daily News*, October 24, 2004. Retrieved January 24, 2009 (http://www.nydailynews.com/archives/sports/2004/10/24/2004-10-24_get_a_grip_tiki_tired_of_hea.html).

Wynne, Sharon Kennedy. "Ronde and Tiki Barber 'Go Long' in Kids Book." *St. Petersburg Times*, September 23, 2008. Retrieved January 6, 2009 (http://www.tampabay.com/features/parenting/article824166.ece).

Zinzer, Lynn. "Pro Football; An Unbreakable Twin Formation." *New York Times*, October 5, 2003. Retrieved January 29, 2009 (http://query.nytimes.com/gst/fullpage.html?sec=health&res=9D03E4DF133CF936A35753C1A9659C8B63).

INDEX

ABOUT THE AUTHOR

Bridget Heos played college football . . . in a dorm league. She was voted best defensive player by the only two fans who ever came to a game. Football is big in her family. Her dad and younger brother coached, and her dad and older brother played college ball. Now her sons play. She is the author of five children's books and hundreds of articles for newspapers and magazines. She lives in Kansas City with her husband and three sons.

PHOTO CREDITS

Designer: Les Kanturek; Editor: Bethany Bryan;
Photo Researcher: Marty Levick